OVER 25 YEARS AFTER THE FALL
BERLIN WALL
marques vickers
TRACKING THE REMANTS

THE BERLIN WALL: Over 25 Years After The Fall

Tracking the Remnants

MARQUIS PUBLISHING
HERRON ISLAND, WASHINGTON

TABLE OF CONTENTS

Edition 1

Published by Marquis Publishing
Herron Island, Washington

Vickers, Marques, 1957

THE BERLIN WALL: Over 25 Years After The Fall
Tracking the Remnants

To My Daughters Charline and Caroline. To Adrian Wilkes and Lisa Vickers-Wilkes for generously hosting me during my visit.

Preface

Artificially constructed Walls are inherently divisive. If the legacy of the Berlin Wall is closely scrutinized, the objective behind its creation was a failure. There are no simplistic answers to immigration control. The oppressed and disadvantaged seek to better their lives in more affluence environments. Many will pursue whatever path is available at the risk of capture, imprisonment or death.

Tracking The Remnants: The Remains of the Berlin Wall Over 25 Years After the Fall

It is difficult to return to events and junctures in history and fully comprehend all of the contributing factors that resulted in consequential decisions. The element of historical immediacy has receded. The verbal and written exchanges, negotiations and compromises may have been thoroughly scrutinized, however often the results remain baffling.

I have always questioned why the Allied nations enabled the Soviet Union to dominate Eastern Europe and particularly East Germany following the conclusion of World War II. Certainly we were aware of the devil represented in the guise of Joseph Stalin. Certainly Russia was motivated by remorseless revenge following Germany's own invasion and destruction of their territories. Yet Russia was not alone in suffering significant loss.

A maxim regarding history seems appropriate. Winners write historical accounts and losers absorb the consequences.

The Western nation's permissiveness towards the predator Soviet Union shackled half of Europe into forced subservience and submissiveness for over forty-five years. Questions still linger as to whether this influence will ever be eradicated.

The Partition of Two Germanys in 1945

In the instance of the German nation, how does a warring party adequately atone for and address their heinous and criminal past? The Third Reich government of Adolph Hitler was responsible for a global warfare and civilian genocide whose scale was unprecedented in history.

The Soviet imposed punishment of post-war Germany suppressed any movement towards democracy. The repercussions exacted a decapitating price on the evolution of Eastern Europe. Within Germany, the western sector elevated itself into prosperity. The agrarian and decimated eastern sector languished in ruin and poverty. The Berlin Wall epitomized the most iconic expression for this repression.

Why Was the Wall Constructed?

The Wall's creation was not immediate following the conclusion of World War II. Construction commenced twelve years later in August 1961 following a sustained population exodus from the eastern German Democratic Republic (GDR).

The GDR was a failed experiment from the outset. The country officially became a nation in 1949. A Berlin worker's uprising in 1953 immediately tested the Soviet occupation. An unrelenting depopulation of the country via the portal of Berlin necessitated drastic action. Within the first twelve years of existence, over twenty percent of the population had been drained.

More telling, the departure of skilled laborers and professionals created serious worker shortages and a substantial stagnation of progress and development. During the summer of 1961, an estimated 1,000 people a day were defecting via the divided capital. Berlin was geographically stranded within the GDR, but offered direct and free access to the rest of West Germany. This incentive stimulated relocation from the east on a massive scale.

Abrupt and Unforeseen Construction

On August 13, 1961, East Berlin residents awoke to barbed

wire fencing that had been installed dividing the city's east and west sectors. Dual concrete barricades incrementally fortified this temporary barrier. The Berlin Wall rose nearly twelve feet in height and extended in excess of 27 miles within Berlin. Over its entirety, the Wall stretched 96 miles segregating the countryside between the GDR and Federal Republic of Germany.

From a propaganda perspective, the GDR hailed the construction as a preventative measure against western intrusion. East German residents understood better.

How The Wall's Layout Was Composed

The Berlin Wall was actually composed of two separate dividing segments, buffered by an empty strip of barren land between. This *No Man's Land* or vortex of death for escape attempts contained hundreds of watchtowers, trenches, guard dog patrols, floodlights and trip-activated machine guns.

Despite these extreme preventative measures, an estimated 5,000 individuals claimed to have escaped by scaling or tunneling underneath. At least 138 people were confirmed dead upon their attempts to cross. Most were shot. The initial 1961 fatality was a woman who leapt from her fourth-floor apartment window while construction began below. The final death, seven months before the permanent breech, was a man whose hot air balloon crashed into power lines.

Such extreme measures symbolized the varied and desperate nature of escape attempts.

Tracing the Remnants of the Wall

This edition visually tracks the Wall's path over twenty-five years following its permanent closure. The journey portrays the traditional and contemporary cultural, legislative, commercial and residential arteries of Berlin. The Wall forcibly severed development in these territories for thirty-eight years.

Contemporary Berlin scarcely resembles the divided and scarred version of 1989. The reunification of Germany expediently and aesthetically repaired infrastructure, upgraded design and created a dynamic creative synergy. The process is not fully complete, but significantly evident since my prior visit in 1996. Nostalgia appears absent for a return to a divided city.

The tracing of the Wall remains a shadowy stigma. Sporadic intact sections remain. More commonly, double lines of rectangular cobblestones signify its former path.

Commercial and residential development has remained impervious to this former outline. Cars routinely park atop and pedestrians routinely stroll upon the stones oblivious to their former significance. Its once profaned presence has become nearly invisible. This invisibility and irreverence towards tradition is desirable. Ghosts and phantoms only haunt those whom they empower.

I discovered only one remaining half-block stretch of Wall absent of development within the city core.

Unified Berlin is not a mausoleum of antiquated remembrance. The city radiates vibrancy. It has successfully integrated the shame of historical actions, consequences and memorials into its present tense. The majority of new constructions are located within the former territories of East Berlin. That land was essentially vacant in 1989 when the Wall officially fell. Due to its previous proximity to the Wall, the real estate then was significantly undervalued. This valuation discrepancy no longer exists.

Prominent Memorials of Remembrance

Can there ever exist adequate compensation and observance sufficient to address global evil?

The answer remains subjective. The level of direct impact on each observer influences his or her view. For those most impacted, sculpture, statuary and traveling exhibitions will always remain insufficient.

For the billions of individuals conceived since the conclusion of World War II, the atrocities seemingly lessen in immediacy and significance with each passing year. It is difficult to imagine that our world may one day minimize such a monumental and catastrophic tragedy. Yet someday perhaps to some successive generation, the events of the Holocaust, World War II and the Cold War era may be simply consigned as historical examples of war and failed conquest.

Heaven prevent that *someday* from ever arriving.

A Voyage Encompassing From North to South Berlin

Our Wall tracking begins in the southwestern extremity of Wedding, a borough of northwestern Berlin. This sector was fused with the Tiergarten and Mitte districts during the city's 2001 administrative reform. Wedding has traditionally been considered one of the poorest immigrant neighborhoods. During the late 1920s, violent clashes between the strong militant Communist population and Nazi sympathizers were common. Residents seeking to compete economically with the more affluence city districts have since displaced clashes over political ideologies.

Gartenstrasse Wall and Bridge

A tan graffitied wall lines Gartenstrasse Road. The orderly bricks appear in contrast to the stark reinforced cement slabs that composed the Berlin Wall. Darker accent bricks crown the barrier that formerly insulated S-Bahn trains operating on two separate elevated steel girder bridges above the roadway. The eastern span no longer operates. The decaying structure has been abandoned to corroding elements, overgrowth and vandalism. Fencing blocks access to the rails. The western span is fully operational on a daily schedule.

The southern extremity of Gartenstrasse Road intersects with Bernauer Strasse Road. This conjunction is noteworthy for a 1961 completed, but scarcely used East German refugee tunnel. A section of the Berlin Wall was relocated atop the tunnel's terminus opening.

Liesenstrasse Wall and Cemetery Row

The Wall veered west onto Lisenstrasse Road. Vaulted above a more battered segment of the Gartenstrasse wall is a section of spray painted concrete slab. The exterior exhibits post-1989 graffiti. Strands of structural rebar protrude from the exterior. This segment reveals punctures through the concrete.

Mitte District: Liesenstrasse, Boyenstrasse and Chausseestrasse Streets

The Wall along Lisenstrasse Road borders four successive cemeteries: Kirchhote, St. Hedwig, Berl Domgemeinde and Franzusischen. Positioned beneath the Wall's former shadow, each becomes a poignant reminder of loss. The burial grounds are suitably maintained minus extravagance.

The Wall then connected with Boyenstrasse and Chausseestrasse Roads, part of the northwestern Mitte district. These neighborhoods feature primarily modern commercial and residential developments. Most are located within the former East Berlin. On the western side of Boyenstrasse, an expansive wooded park and athletic complex features a soccer field, ice-skating rink and tennis courts.

Scharnhorststrasse Street and Spandauer Canal
Easing southward onto Scharnhorststrasse Street, the Wall follows the contours of the Spandauer Canal that formed a natural border. Spandauer empties into the Humboldthafen Canal. Scharnhorststrasse Streets terminates at the intersection of Invalidenstrasse Road. The German Ministry of Economics and Energy Building and Invalidity Park are located on separate northern corners.

Invalides Cemetery
In between the ending point are the grounds of the famed Invalides Cemetery, one of the oldest in Berlin. The cemetery was established in 1748 to bury Prussian distinguished army nobility and soldiers. By 1872, 18,000 funerals had taken place on the grounds. Numerous commanders who fought in World War I including Hoffmann, von Moltke and von Falkenhausen are buried in the cemetery. The remains of Manfred von Richthofen, the *Red Baron*, were transferred from France in 1925.

Several tombs of Nazi era figures existed before the cemetery's official closure in 1951. The Allies ordered all of the Nazi monuments to be removed, but the buried remains were left intact. A third of the cemetery was destroyed with the creation of the Berlin Wall and accompanying watchtowers, barracks, roads and parking lots. Some of the graves suffered shrapnel damage from gunfire exchanges originating from the guard towers.

German Ministry of Economics and Energy Building and The Invalidity Park
The Ministry of Economics and Energy Building located at the southern end of Scharnhorststrasse dates from the early twentieth century with more recent additions to the expanded complex. Invalidity Park features a sunken Wall Memorial eulogizing the former Gnadenkirche church destroyed during World War II and the Berlin Wall.

Humboldthafen Canal and Gunter Litfin
Upon crossing the bridge at Invalidenstrasse Road and heading southward, the Wall proceeded along Alexanderufer Street. The Spandauer emptied into the Humboldthafen Canal just below a railroad crossing bridge. These waters were the location of one of the first aborted escapes during the construction of the Wall. Gunter Litfin, 24, was a tailor who was already working in West Berlin. He had found a new apartment and was in the process of finalizing his move on August 13, 1961.

Roadblocks and barbwire were stretched that day. His plans to return were delayed. On the late afternoon of August 24th, he attempted to cross the canal by swimming a narrow channel. East German transportation police discovered his crossing. He was ordered to swim back. He reportedly lifted his hands from the water and was shot dead. He was the second official crossing casualty and the first to be killed by gunfire.

Museum of Medical History at the Charity
The Wall followed the course of the Humboldthafen Canal. The Museum of Medical History rests adjacently on Alexanderufer Street. The architecture is predominantly late 19th century red brick. The museum was formerly the Berlin Pathological Institute. Its permanent exhibition

traces medical history over the past 300 years. An enormous specimen hall features over 750 pathologic and anatomical wet and dry preparations for display. University courses are still conducted on the grounds.

Alexanderufer Street, Humboldthafen Canal and Hauptbahnhof Railway Station

Continuing further along Alexanderufer, a contemporary office complex straddles the Wall's divide. To the west, across the Humboldthafen Canal, the modernized Hauptbahnhof Railway Station is visible. A 2006 upgrade expanded it from a smaller S-Bahn station. Today Hauptbahnhof operates as Berlin's central railway station.

Schiffbauerdamm Street

The Wall shifted along Schiffbauerdamm Street southward in a rounded arch before crossing over the Spree River at the Wilhelmstrasse Road Bridge. Wedged into the convergence of the bridge and Schiffbauerdamm is the striking Marie-Elisabeth Luders building located along the river embankment and fronting Luisenstraase Road. The structure operates as the scientific service and infrastructure center of Germany's Parliament. Marie-Elisabeth Luders was the former chairwoman of the German Bundestag.

German Reichstag and Parliament Buildings

The Wall headed west towards Friedrich Ebert Platz passing in front of the German Reichstag Building. Current parliament and governmental buildings have been constructed atop former Wall placements.

The Reichstag building housed the historical Imperial Government of the German Empire dating back to 1894. It was used as the seat of government until a mysterious 1933 fire, presumably set by the Nazi's. The building was further damaged during World War II. Nearly resting against the

Wall in West German territory, it remained abandoned and in disuse.

The building and its infamous past were left to fester. A major restoration project followed German reunification. The building was officially reopened to acclaim in October 1999. It currently functions as the principle meeting site for the German Parliament.

Eastern Tiergarten

The Wall headed southbound along Friedrick Ebertstrasse Road continuing across the street from the Reichstag. It resumed towards the Brandenburg Gate. On Ebertstrasse's western flank is Berlin's enormous Tiergarten Park. The Park extends eastward until reaching Potsdamer Platz. The grounds feature a zoo, expansive woodlands, ponds, streams and monuments throughout. The eastern portion that directly faced the Wall today features numerous commemoratives. Among them include a white cross procession of refugee casualties from the GDR, a statue of writer Johann Wolfgang von Goethe and a memorial to Homosexuals Persecuted Under Nazism.

Pariser Platz

Pariser Platz is located to the east and across the street from the northern tip of the Tiergarten. A small portion runs southward on Frederick Ebertstrasse Platz until reaching the plaza of the Brandenburg Gate. The Platz surface area continues behind the Gate. Its crescent shape includes the American and French Embassies, Berlin Academy of Arts, and diverse banking, retail and commercial institutions.

The former structures encompassing the Pariser Plaza were reduced to rubble during World War II. Their staggering shells remained unrestored for decades by the GDR due to their close proximity to the Wall. Restoration began immediately in 1990.

Brandenburg Gate

The Brandenburg Gate is an 18th century neoclassical monument serving as an entry to *Unter den Linden*, the boulevard of linden trees. This road historically led to the Prussian Palace of Monarchs. Prussian King Frederick William II commissioned the edifice in 1788 as a sign of peace. The message, by contrast, radiates military triumph. The monument suffered considerable damage during World War II. The Gate laid in a perpetual state of disrepair on the eastern side of the Wall until the reunification process commenced renovations in 2000.

The Memorial to the Murdered Jews of Europe

Continuing southward along Friedrick Ebertstrasse Road, an unconventional monument was established in 2004 as a memorial to European Jewish victims from the Holocaust. Large rectangular concrete slabs simulating cemetery tombs are arranged in a grid pattern on a sloping field and vary in heights. The enormity of 2,700 slabs represents the magnitude and scale of the crime and killings.

Site of Adolph Hitler's Bunker

Approximately one block southeast from the Wall and Holocaust Memorial is the former site of Adolph Hitler's bunker complex. The intricate structure was constructed between 1936-1944 during the height of the war. The former air raid shelter was Hitler's final Nazi command post and the site where he committed suicide with his new bride Eva Braun during the last week of April 1945. The occupying Soviet Union forces leveled the structure immediately following the war. Limited excavation began during the reconstruction of the neighborhood. Today the location is a bare land space and paved parking lot for a multi-level residential development.

Ebertstrasse Boulevard Office and Retail

Resuming the Wall's routing southwards towards Potsdamer Platz, both sides of Ebertstrasse feature increasing additions of office and commercial projects. These buildings spill onto Potsdamer and Leipziger Platz.

Potsdamer Platz

Potsdamer Platz is currently a highly frequented public square that obtained its name from where the old Potsdam city road passed through the city wall of Berlin. During World War II, the area was completely decimated and remained desolate throughout the Cold War era. Following reunification and beginning in 1995, Potsdamer became the most concentrated site for major skyscraper construction and commercial development.

Leipziger Platz

The octagonal shaped square is located in the Mitte district across the road from the former Wall and Potsdamer Platz. Leipziger Platz was originally developed between 1732 and 1738. During its heightened prestige, it boasted some of Berlin's most sought after residential, administrative and commercial buildings. During the World War II bombings, these structures were obliterated. During the Cold War, the plaza remained in ruins. Since reunification, construction activity has mirrored Potsdamer Platz. Multi-level commercial and office structures line the octagon and feature the subterranean Mall of Berlin shopping center.

Stresemannstrasse Street Office Buildings

Exiting Potsdamer and Leipziger Platz, the Wall curved along southbound Stresemannstrasse Street. Today multi-level commercial and office complexes line the corridor. The Wall continued eastward along Niederkirchnersrasse

Street, the location of the Lantag of Prussia Building, Martin-Gropius-Bau Museum and Topography of Terror Museum.

The Lantag of Prussia Building

The Lantag of Prussia housed the representative assembly of the Kingdom of Prussia beginning in 1899. During December 1918, the German National Workers and Soldiers Council held their assemblies within the building. On January 1, 1919, their deliberations resulted in the founding of the German Communist Party. During World War II, the building served as an annex for Hermann Goring's Ministry of Aviation. Upon the establishment of the GDR, the site housed numerous departments for the Academy of Sciences. Economic five-year plans for the GDR were formulated in the conference rooms. Since 2000, the building has served as the seat for the German Bundesrat, a legislative body that represents the sixteen federal states of Germany at the national level.

Martin-Gropius-Bau Museum

The Martin-Gropius-Bau Museum was constructed in 1881 in the neo-Renaissance style with a quadratic ground plan. The exhibition rooms surround a grandiose atrium decorated with mosaics and the coats of arms representing the German states. The structure was heavily damaged at the conclusion of World War II. During the Cold War era, the building rested on the border between East and West Berlin as the boundary of the East's Mitte district. It reopened in 1981 following three years of post-war reconstruction. The building is considered one of Germany's finest and most picturesque exhibition halls.

Topography of Terror Museum

The Topography of Terror Museum is an outdoor and indoor reminder of the carnage and human loss responsible by the Nazi regime. The two most striking elements are the expansive remnants of the Wall and the foundational remains of the former Gestapo headquarters. The Wall segment stretches halfway along Niederkirchnersrasse Street between the Documentation Building of the museum and The Lantag of Prussia Building. During the Cold War era, the street was a heavily fortified boundary between conflicting philosophies.

This Wall segment is the longest remaining shared portion viewable formerly by both sides. The East Side Gallery remains the most expansive intact segment. During the Cold War, that portion was not visible to the West, obscured by the Spree River.

Allied bombing during early 1945 destroyed the Gestapo and SS headquarters. What remained was demolished during post-war reconstruction in the west. The cellar of the infamous Gestapo headquarters was discovered and excavated in 1987. Cooperating West and East German researchers conducted the project.

The Gestapo building was where political prisoners were tortured and often executed. Following the joint country excavation, the exposed foundation walls were turned into an open-air memorial and protected by a canopy. Today, the remains are pedestrian accessible and protected by a steel frame and glass covering.

The final construction of the adjacent Documentation Center shared its own tortuous history. The building project began during 1994, but was halted due to funding problems upon the completion of the concrete core. For a decade construction remained in suspension until the base was demolished. Another design was accepted and the current structure was completed in 2010. The Center's exhibitions offer exhaustive visual and reprinted documentation tracing the violent rise of the Nazi party, persecution of the Jewish race and minorities, and the Holocaust terror.

Checkpoint Charlie

The Wall continued one block east to the intersection of Freidrichstrasse and Zimmerstrasse. This intersection supported the border crossing known as Checkpoint Charlie. American occupation forces coined the designation based on the phonetic alphabet. Two other border crossings were named Alpha and Bravo. The unassuming guardhouse was the only gateway where East Germany allowed Allied diplomats, military personnel and foreign tourists to pass into Berlin's Soviet sector.

The original 1961 temporary station was replaced several times by structures of different sizes and layouts. The final 1990 guardhouse was relocated for display in an open-air museum of the Allied Museum in Berlin-Zehlendorf. The currently stationed facsimile is a hybrid of former versions and includes stacked sandbags that many did not.

Zimmerstrasse Road

The Wall continued eastward stretching along Zimmerstrasse Road. Recent commercial and residential developments have blended in seamlessly with still standing classical Berlin architecture. Zimmerstrasse Road shifts northeast until its termination at Axel-Sprinnerstrasse Road.

Axel Springerstrasse, Kommandantenstrasse and Alte Jakobstrasse

The wall zigzagged through the commercial and residential sectors of Axel Springerstrasse, Kommandantenstrasse and Alte Jakobstrasse Streets. Development have replaced this former desolate *No Man's Land.*

Stallschreiberstrasse Street No Mans Land

At the intersection of Alte Jakobstrasse and Stallschreiberstrasse, residential development is under construction fronting the northern half of Stallschreiberstrasse Street. Continuing south is a half-block strip of No Man's Land. This area represents the final undeveloped Wall terrain within the core of Berlin.

Where the Wall was removed decades ago, a harmless well-trodden pathway continues until Alexandriastrasse Street. The banality of the open landscape makes its former menace imperceptible.

Soon this bare stretch will exist no longer. Pristine and durable sewage pipes are preparing the neighborhood for additional residential construction. Progress prevails where blood was once absorbed into the soil.

Alexandriastrasse, Sebastianstrasse and Luckauerstrasse Streets

The Wall continued its circuitous path absorbing Alexandriastrasse, Sebastianstrasse and Luckauerstrasse Streets. Fresh residential buildings have been constructed. Street signage designates a few of the older houses as former eastern escape passages. Most escapes were unsuccessful and discovered before being employed. The hardest task involved in escape was silence and avoiding denouncements by curious and patriotic neighbors.

The once elegant 19th century Sebastianstrasse stone mansions mask the fate of lost lives and aborted tunnels beneath. Today we may freely cross this death strip without caution or consequence.

Waldemarstrasse and Leuschnerdamm Streets

At the intersection of Luckauerstrasse and Dresdenerstrasse Streets, the Wall continued to Waldemarstrasse Street. Waldemarstrasse is residential and the gateway to stately Engelbecken Park.

Engelbecken Park and Luisenstadt Canal

Engelbecken Park (Angel's Pool) is an accumulation pond for the former Luisenstadt Canal. Branching off from Waldemarstrasse Street, Legiendamm and Leuschnerdamm Roads veer parallel into a chalice shape and surround the modest ornamental pool. These stilled waters are all that remain of the former mile and a half artery that once linked the Landwehr Canal to the south and Spree River to the northeast.

The Luisenstadt Canal was constructed between 1848 and 1852 and used for water transport and land drainage. From the outset, its served as a design and decorative strip, flanked by quays with neoclassical architecture. Low water flows resulted in ongoing stagnation. Eventually the Canal was transformed into extensive sunken gardens. Between 1926 and 1932, the canal was filled in permanently. These parklands and gardens strips stretch along the northern curvature of Engeldamm Road.

St. Michael's Church

North of the Engelbecken pool is Kaiser-Franz-Grenadier Platz and Saint Michael's Church. Saint Michael's is a Roman Catholic ruin that was heavily damaged during the World War II bombings. Like most ecclesiastical structures during the Cold War era, it was only partially repaired. It remains primarily a skeleton and is desperate in need of sponsorship and repair funding.

The church was dedicated to the Archangel Michael and completed in 1851. It has often been compared with the architect's vision of the Venetian church of San Giorgio Maggiore. The structure features three apses and a vast nave area. The majority of the sanctuary remains open, vacant and vulnerable to the elements.

Critics once regarded the completed jewel as a successful synthesis between classical and medieval architecture. Today the questions remains, can it be successfully regenerated?

Engeldamm Street and the Luisenstadt Canal Gardens
At the intersection of Leuschnerdamm and Engeldamm Roads, the Wall curved in a northeastwardly arch ultimately leading to a bridge spanning the Spree River. Between Engeldamm and the parallel routed Bethaniendamm Road, the Luisenstadt Canal gardens were converted into a green path separating the two roadways. Both avenues are located within the former East Berlin.

During the Cold War era, the gardens served as a secondary buffer zone fronting the Wall. Neoclassical houses line the more elevated Engeldamm Road. Mariannenplatz parklands and St. Thomas' Church were positioned to the southwest on the West German portion of the Wall.

St. Thomas' Church and Mariannenplatz
St. Thomas' Church was constructed between 1865 and 1869. Prior to the completion of the Berliner Dom, it was the largest Protestant church in Berlin. At its zenith, its congregation was one of the largest in Western Europe.

Mariannenplatz features expansive park grounds. On the northeastern periphery formerly bordering the Wall, several neoclassical buildings remain in varied states of reparation.

An apparent squatter's community co-exists next to the restoration efforts. Their long-term existence may become contentious with continued escalating real estate values and civic housing demands.

Stralauer Platz and Muhlenstrasse Streets

The Spree River in several instances formed a natural barrier between the two Berlins. Crossing northward over the Engeldamm Bridge, the Wall traced an eastward path along Stralauer Platz and Muhlenstrasse Streets. The existing structures lining both roads are principally industrial structures. They front Berlin's East Train Station that has been completely renovated. Commercial developments are being incrementally added along the shoreline. The removal of the Wall today enables an unobstructed view towards West Berlin.

East Side Gallery

Continuing along Muhlenstrasse Street, the longest stretch of the remaining Wall (4,300+ feet) has been converted into an international outdoor art gallery. Graffiti art has adorned the bare and defaced concrete since 1990. The original artists periodically refreshen their designs. Ongoing competitions keep the imagery fresh, but in many instances are overwritten by unsanctioned graffiti improvisers.

Oberbaum Bridge

Muhlenstrasse Street terminates at the Oberbaum Bridge. The span crosses the Spree River back to West Berlin. This double-deck bridge was originally constructed in 1732 connecting the municipality of Berlin with the then outlying rural area. The name *Ober* is translated into upper and *Baum* refers to the heavy tree trunks that once blocked the river at night to prevent smuggling. The original viaduct featured a prominent drawbridge. During the Cold War era, the bridge connected two divided Berlin boroughs. The lower deck of the bridge currently features a vehicle and pedestrian crossing. The upper level carries the U-Bahn rail line.

Stralauer Allee Road Industrial Sector

The Wall continued eastward along Stralauer Allee Road employing the Spree River as a natural barrier. The land utilization then as now is predominately industrial. As with our starting point of Wedding, lower priced rents and housing attract a more economically fringed residential base. The least developed land parcels of contemporary Berlin exist within this territorial zoning.

This too shall change with time.

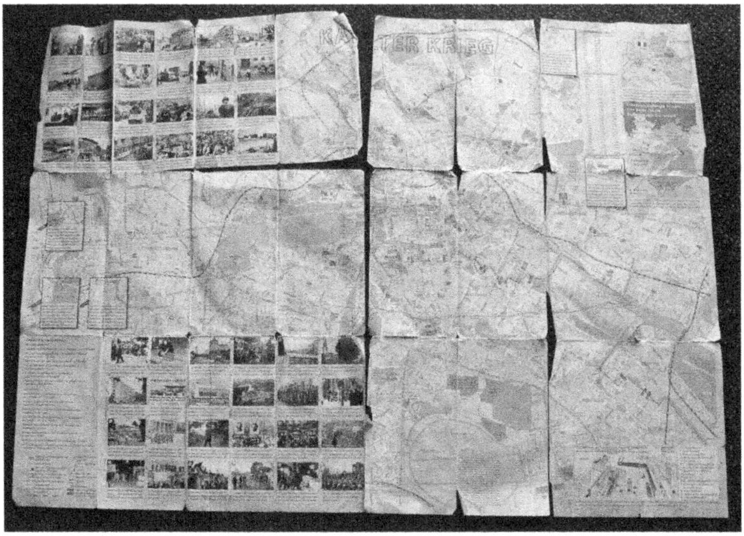

Gartenstrasse Road Wall (East Berlin)

Eastern Span of Gartenstrasse Rd Bridge

Blocked Off Span Gartenstrasse Road Bridge

Eastern Section of the Gartenstrasse Road Bridge

Blocked Off Span Gartenstrasse Road Bridge

Lisenstrasse Rd Wall Remnant (East Berlin)

Lisenstrasse Rd Wall Remnant (East)

Lisenstrasse Road Cemetaries (East Berlin)

Liesenstrasse Road Cemetary (East Berlin)

Liesenstrasse Road Cemetary (East)

Liesenstrasse Road Cemetary (East Berlin)

Cemetery Monument

Mitte District Developments (East Berlin)

Mitte District Developments (East)

Mitte District Developments (West Berlin)

Mitte District Developments (West Berlin)

Boyenstrasse Road Park (West Berlin)

Mitte District Development (East Berlin)

Mittre District Development (East Berlin)

Mitte District Development (East)

Mitte District Development (East Berlin)

Mitte District Development (East Berlin)

Mitte District Development (East Berlin)

Trail of the Berlin Wall

Mitte District Development (East Berlin)

Mitte District Development (East Berlin)

Mitte District Development (East Berlin)

Mitte District Development (East Berlin)

Athletic Facility Ice Skating Rink (West Berlin)

Mitte District Development (East Berlin)

Scharnhorststrasse Development (East)

Bundeswehr Hospital (East Berlin)

Scharnhorststrasse Building (East Berlin)

Scharnhorststrasse Development (East Berlin)

Scharnhorststrasse Buildings (East Berlin)

Scharnhorststrasse Development (East Berlin)

Scharnhorststrasse Developments (East)

Scharnhorststrasse Development (East Berlin)

Scharnhorststrasse Building (East Berlin)

Scharnhorststrasse Building (East Berlin)

View to West Berlin next to Spandauer Canal

View to West Berlin next to Spandauer Canal

Invalides Cemetery (East Berlin)

Invalides Cemetery (East Berlin)

Invalides Cemetery (East Berlin)

Invalides Cemetery (East Berlin)

Invalides Cemetery (East Berlin)

Ministry of Economics and Energy Building (East Berlin)

Ministry of Economics and Energy Building (East Berlin)

Ministry of Economics and Energy Building (East Berlin)

Ministry of Economics and Energy Building (East Berlin)

The Invalidity Park (East Berlin)

The Invalidity Park (East Berlin)

The Invalidity Park (East Berlin)

Museum of Medical History (East Berlin)

Museum of Medical History (East Berlin)

Museum of Medical History (East Berlin)

Museum of Medical History (East Berlin)

Museum of Medical History (East Berlin)

Museum of Medical History (East Berlin)

View of West Berlin Across Humboldthafen Canal

Hauptbahnhof Railway Station

View of Hauptbahnhof Railway Station

Hauptbahnhof Railway Station

View Below Rail Bridge

Alexanderufer Office Complex

Alexanderufer Office Complex

Alexanderufer Office Complex

Alexanderufer Office Complex

Alexanderufer Office Complex

Schiffbauerdamm Street Office Complex (East Berlin)

Schiffbauerdamm Street Office Complexes (East Berlin)

Schiffbauerdamm Street Office Complexes (East Berlin)

Schiffbauerdamm Street Office Complex (East Berlin)

Bridge Crossing the River Spree

Along the Spree River

Marie-Elisabeth Luders Building (East Berlin)

Marie-Elisabeth Luders Building (East Berlin)

Marie-Elisabeth Luders Building (East Berlin)

Marie-Elisabeth Luders Building (East Berlin)

Marie-Elisabeth Luders Building (East Berlin)

Marie-Elisabeth Luders Building (East Berlin)

Views From the Wilhelmstrasse Road Bridge (West Berlin)

View From Wilhelmstrasse Rd Bridge

Views From Wilhelmstrasse Road Bridge (East Berlin)

Bridge Spanning Spree River

The German Reichstag (West Berlin)

The German Reichstag (West Berlin)

The German Reichstag (West Berlin)

The German Reichstag (West Berlin)

Friedrich Ebert Platz Office Building (East Berlin)

Friedrich Ebert Platz Government Building (East Berlin)

Friedrich Ebert Platz Government Building (East Berlin)

Friedrich Ebert Platz Government Building (East Berlin)

Friedrich Ebert Platz Office Building (East Berlin)

Friedrich Ebert Platz Government Building (East Berlin)

Friedrich Ebert Platz Government Buildings (East Berlin)

Friedrich Ebert Platz Government Buildings (East Berlin)

Eastern Sector of Tiergarten Park (West Berlin)

White Cross Memorials for GDR Victims (West Berlin)

Memorial to Homosexuals Persecuted Under Nazism (West Berlin)

Eastern Sector of Tiergarten Park (West Berlin)

Monument to Johann Wolfgang von Goethe (West)

Approaching Pariser Platz From North (East)

Approaching Pariser Platz From South (East)

View from Pariser Platz (East Berlin)

Facing Pariser Platz (East Berlin)

Southern Sector of Pariser Platz (East Berlin)

South and Southeast Behind Pariser Platz (East)

Northern Sector of Pariser Platz (East Berlin)

Interior Office Courtyard (East Berlin)

Brandenburg Gate (East Berlin Sector)

Brandenburg Gate (East Berlin Sector)

Brandenburg Gate (East Berlin Sector)

Brandenburg Gate (East Berlin Sector)

Brandenburg Gate (East Berlin Sector)

Brandenburg Gate (East Berlin Sector)

The Memorial to the Murdered Jews of Europe (East Berlin)

The Memorial to the Murdered Jews of Europe (East Berlin)

The Memorial to the Murdered Jews of Europe (East Berlin)

The Memorial to the Murdered Jews of Europe (East Berlin)

The Memorial to the Murdered Jews of Europe (East Berlin)

The Memorial to the Murdered Jews of Europe (East Berlin)

Adolph Hitler's Bunker Site (East Berlin)

Adolph Hitler's Bunker Site (East Berlin)

Ebertstrasse Boulevard Office Building (East Berlin)

Ebertstrasse Boulevard Office Building (East Berlin)

Ebertstrasse Boulevard Office and Retail Buildings (East Berlin)

Ebertstrasse Boulevard Office and Retail Building (West Berlin)

Ebertstrasse Boulevard Office and Hotel Buildings (West Berlin)

Straddling the Remnants of the Wall

Potsdamer Platz (East and West Berlin)

Potsdamer Platz (West Berlin)

Potsdamer Platz (West Berlin)

Potsdamer Platz (East and West Berlin)

Potsdamer Platz (East and West Berlin)

Potsdamer Platz (West and East Berlin)

Potsdamer Platz (West Berlin)

Leipziger Platz (East Berlin)

Leipziger Platz (East Berlin)

Leipziger Platz (East Berlin)

Leipziger Platz (East Berlin)

Leipziger Platz (East Berlin)

Stresemannstrasse Street Office Building (East Berlin)

Stresemannstrasse Street Office Building (East Berlin)

Stresemannstrasse Street Wall Stones

Stresemannstrasse Street Office Building (East Berlin)

Stresemannstrasse Street Pagoda (East Berlin)

Stresemannstrasse Street Office Buildings (East Berlin)

Stresemannstrasse Street Office Building (East Berlin)

The Lantag of Prussia Building (East Berlin)

The Lantag of Prussia Building (East Berlin)

The Lantag of Prussia Building (East Berlin)

Lantag of Prussia Building (East Berlin)

Martin-Gropius-Bau Museum (East and West Border)

Martin-Gropius-Bau Museum (East and West Berlin)

Martin-Gropius-Bau Museum (East and West Berlin)

Martin-Gropius-Bau Museum (East and West Berlin)

Remains of the Gestapo Building (West Berlin)

Remains of Gestapo Building (West)

Remains of the Gestapo Building (West Berlin)

Remains of the Gestapo Building (West)

Remains of the Gestapo Building (West Berlin)

Remains of the Gestapo Building (West Berlin)

Topography of Terror Museum (West Berlin)

Topography of Terror Museum (West Berlin)

Remnant of the Wall (West Berlin)

Remnant of the Wall (West Berlin)

Remnant of the Wall (West Berlin)

Remnant of the Wall (West Berlin)

Remnant of the Wall (West Berlin)

Remnant of the Wall (East Berlin)

Remnant of the Wall (West Berlin)

Remnant of the Wall (West Berlin)

Remnants of the Wall (East Berlin)

Checkpoint Charlie Guard Station (East and West Border)

Checkpoint Charlie Guard Station (East and West Berlin)

Checkpoint Charlie Museum (East and West Berlin)

Checkpoint Charlie Museum (East and West Berlin)

Checkpoint Charlie Museum (East and West Berlin)

Zimmerstrasse Street Residential Building (East Berlin)

Zimmerstrasse Street Residential Building (East Berlin)

Zimmerstrasse Street Commercial Buildings (East Berlin)

Zimmerstrasse Street Commercial Building (East Berlin)

Zimmerstrasse Street Commercial Buildings (East Berlin)

Trabant Museum, Zimmerstrasse Street (East Berlin)

Zimmerstrasse Street Wall Remnant

Zimmerstrasse Street Commercial Buildings (East Berlin)

Zimmerstrasse Street Commercial Buildings (East Berlin)

Zimmerstrasse Street Commercial Residential Buildings (East Berlin)

Zimmerstrasse Street Commercial Buildings (East Berlin)

Zimmerstrasse Street Commercial Buildings (East Berlin)

Zimmerstrasse Street Commercial Buildings (East Berlin)

Zimmerstrasse Street Commercial Building (East Berlin)

Zimmerstrasse Street Commercial Buildings (East Berlin)

Zimmerstrasse Street Commercial Buildings (East Berlin)

Zimmerstrasse Street Commercial Building (East Berlin)

Zimmerstrasse Street Commercial Building (East Berlin)

Zimmerstrasse Street Commercial Building (West Berlin)

Axel Springerstrasse Rd. Commerical Building (East Berli

Axel Springerstrasse Road Hotel Property (West Berlin)

Axel Springerstrasse Road Commerical Building (East Berlin)

Axel Springerstrasse Commercial Building (West Berlin)

Axel Springerstrasse Commercial Building (West Berlin)

Axel Springerstrasse Residential Building (East Berlin)

Axel Springerstrasse Road Commerical Building (East Berlin)

Axel Springerstrasse Commercial Building (East Berlin)

Axel Springerstrasse Residential Building (East Berlin)

Kommandantenstrasse Mixed Use Development (East Berlin)

Kommandantenstrasse Road Stones

Kommandantenstrasse Office Building (East Berlin)

Kommandantenstrasse Residential Complex (East)

Kommandantenstrasse Commercial Building (East)

Kommandantenstrasse Commercial Building (West Berlin)

Kommandantenstrasse Residential Building (East Berlin)

Alte Jakobstrasse Residential Building (East Berlin)

Alte Jakobstrasse Residential Building (East Berlin)

Entrance Stallschreiberstrasse Street No Mans Land

View towards the East from No Man's Land

Stallschreiberstrasse Street No Mans Land

Stallschreiberstrasse Street No Mans Land

New Piping Infrastructure Alexandrinenstrasse (East)

Alexandriastrasse Street Residential Building (East Berlin)

Sebastianstrasse Residential Building (East Berlin)

Sebastianstrasse Street Wall Path

Sebastianstrasse Residential Buildings (East Berlin)

Sebastianstrasse Street Residential Building (East Berlin)

Sebastianstrasse Residential Construction (East Berlin)

Sebastianstrasse Residential Building (East Berlin)

Sebastianstrasse Street Residential Complexes (West Berlin)

Sebastianstrasse Trail of the Wall

Sebastianstrasse Residential Building (West Berlin)

Sebastianstrasse Residential Buildings (East Berlin)

Sebastianstrasse St. Former Escape House (East Berlin)

Sebastianstrasse Residential Buildings (West Berlin)

Sebastianstrasse Residential Buildings (West Berlin)

Luckauerstrasse Street Residential Buildings (West Berlin)

Luckauerstrasse Apartment Complex (East Berlin)

Luckauerstrasse Residential Complexes (East Berlin)

Luckauerstrasse Residential Building (West Berlin)

Luckauerstrasse Residential Building (East Berlin)

Luckauerstrasse Street Wall Trail

Waldemarstrasse Residential Buildings (West Berlin)

Waldemarstrasse Residential Buildings (West Berlin)

Leuschnerdamm Walkway to Engelbecken Park (East Berlin)

Engelbecken Park and Ornamental Pool (East Berlin)

Engelbecken Park Gardens (East Berlin)

Engelbecken Park Gardens (East Berlin)

Leuschnerdamm Street Residential Buildings (East Berlin)

Leuschnerdamm Street Residential Buildings (East Berlin)

Leuschnerdamm Street Buildings (East Berlin)

St. Thomas' Church (East Berlin)

St. Thomas' Church (East Berlin)

St. Thomas' Church (East Berlin)

St. Thomas' Church (East Berlin)

St. Thomas' Church (East Berlin)

St. Thomas' Church (East Berlin)

Bethaniendamm Street (East Berlin)

Engeldamm Street (East Berlin)

Drained Luisenstadt Canal Gardens (East Berlin)

Engeldamm Street (East Berlin)

Engeldamm Street (East Berlin)

Bethaniendamm Street (East Berlin)

Engeldamm Street (East Berlin)

Engeldamm Street (East Berlin)

Drained Luisenstadt Canal Gardens (East Berlin)

Drained Luisenstadt Canal Gardens (East Berlin)

Engeldamm Street (East Berlin)

Engeldamm Street (East Berlin)

Engeldamm Street (East Berlin)

Engeldamm Street (East Berlin)

Engeldamm Street (East Berlin)

Engeldamm Street (East Berlin)

Engeldamm Street (East Berlin)

Engeldamm Street (East Berlin)

St. Thomas' Church (West Berlin)

St. Thomas' Church (West Berlin)

Northeastern Periphery of Mariannenplatz(West Berlin)

Northeastern Periphery of Mariannenplatz(West Berlin)

Northeastern Periphery of Mariannenplatz(West Berlin)

Northeastern Periphery of Mariannenplatz(West Berlin)

Northeastern Periphery of Mariannenplatz(West Berlin)

Stralauer Platz Road (East Berlin)

Stralauer Platz Road (East Berlin)

Stralauer Platz Road (East Berlin)

Stralauer Platz Road (East Berlin)

Stralauer Platz Road (East Berlin)

Muhlenstrasse Commercial Building (East Berlin)

View of West Berlin From Across the Spree River

View of West Berlin From Across the Spree River

Muhlenstrasse Street Commercial Building (East Berlin)

Muhlenstrasse Street Commercial Buildings (East Berlin)

Muhlenstrasse Street Commercial Building (East Berlin)

Muhlenstrasse Street Commercial Building (East Berlin)

Former Guard Tower Near Train Station

Muhlenstrasse Street (East Berlin)

Muhlenstrasse Construction (East Berlin)

East Side Gallery (East Berlin)

East Side Gallery (East Berlin)

East Side Gallery (East Berlin)

East Side Gallery (East Berlin)

East Side Gallery (East Berlin)

East Side Gallery (East Berlin)

East Side Gallery (East Berlin)

East Side Gallery (East Berlin)

East Side Gallery (East Berlin)

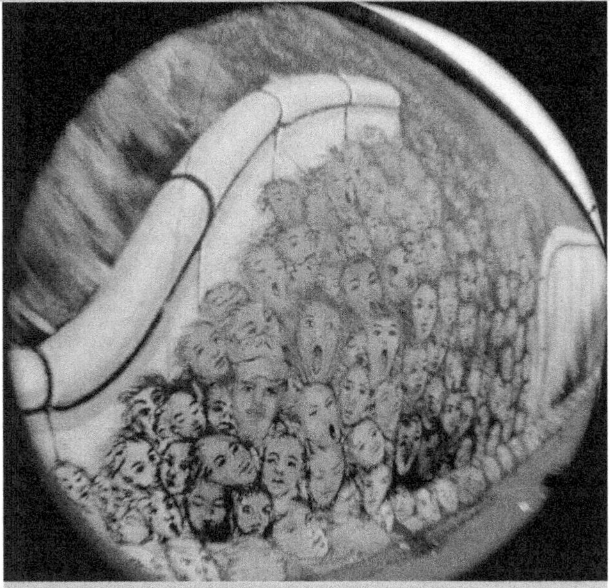

East Side Gallery (East Berlin)

Oberbaum Bridge (East Berlin)

Oberbaum Bridge (East Berlin)

Stralauer Allee Road (East Berlin)

Oberbaum Bridge (East Berlin)

Stralauer Allee Road (East Berlin)

Stralauer Allee Road (East Berlin)

Stralauer Allee Road (East Berlin)

View of West Berlin From Across the Spree River (East Berlin)

Author, photographer and visual artist Marques Vickers was born in 1957 in Vallejo, California. He graduated from Azusa Pacific University in Los Angeles and became the Public Relations and Executive Director for the Burbank, California Chamber of Commerce between 1979-84.

Professionally, he has operated travel, apparel, wine, rare book and publishing businesses. His paintings and sculptures have been exhibited in art galleries, private collections and museums in the United States and Europe. He has previously lived in the Burgundy and Languedoc regions of France and currently lives in the South Puget Sound region of Western Washington.

He has written and published over one hundred books spanning a diverse variety of subjects including true crime, international travel, social satire, wine production, architecture, history, fiction, auctions, fine art, poetry and photojournalism.

He has two daughters, Charline and Caroline who reside in Europe.

Made in the USA
Middletown, DE
08 December 2019

80231306R00116